IF FOUND PLl

👤 _____

✉ _____

📱 _____

Greater Than a Tourist Book Series Reviews from Readers

I think the series is wonderful and beneficial for tourists to get information before visiting the city.

-Seckin Zumbul, Izmir Turkey

I am a world traveler who has read many trip guides but this one really made a difference for me. I would call it a heartfelt creation of a local guide expert instead of just a guide.

-Susy, Isla Holbox, Mexico

New to the area like me, this is a must have!

 -Joe, Bloomington, USA

This is a good series that gets down to it when looking for things to do at your destination without having to read a novel for just a few ideas.

-Rachel, Monterey, USA

Good information to have to plan my trip to this destination.

-Pennie Farrell, Mexico

Great ideas for a port day.

-Mary Martin USA

Aptly titled, you won't just be a tourist after reading this book. You'll be greater than a tourist!

-Alan Warner, Grand Rapids, USA

Even though I only have three days to spend in San Miguel in an upcoming visit, I will use the author's suggestions to guide some of my time there. An easy read - with chapters named to guide me in directions I want to go.

-Robert Catapano, USA

Great insights from a local perspective! Useful information and a very good value!

-Sarah, USA

This series provides an in-depth experience through the eyes of a local. Reading these series will help you to travel the city in with confidence and it'll make your journey a unique one.

-Andrew Teoh, Ipoh, Malaysia

\>TOURIST

GREATER THAN A TOURIST- GETTYSBURG PENNSYLVANIA USA

50 Travel Tips from a Local

Melody Guillen

Greater Than a Tourist- Gettysburg Pennsylvania USA Copyright © 2018 by
CZYK Publishing LLC. All Rights Reserved.

All rights reserved. No part of this book may be reproduced in any form or by
any electronic or mechanical means including information storage and retrieval
systems, without permission in writing from the author. The only exception is by
a reviewer, who may quote short excerpts in a review.

The statements in this book are of the authors and may not be the views of
CZYK Publishing or Greater Than a Tourist.

Cover designed by: Ivana Stamenkovic
Cover Image: https://pixabay.com/en/cannon-history-battle-military-1017749/

CZYK Publishing Since 2011.

Greater Than a Tourist
Visit our website at www.GreaterThanaTourist.com

Lock Haven, PA
All rights reserved.
ISBN: 9781791610371

>TOURIST

50 TRAVEL TIPS FROM A LOCAL

>TOURIST

BOOK DESCRIPTION

Are you excited about planning your next trip?

Do you want to try something new?

Would you like some guidance from a local?

If you answered yes to any of these questions, then this Greater Than a Tourist book is for you.

Greater Than A Tourist - Gettysburg, Pennsylvania USA by Melody Guillen offers the inside scoop on Gettysburg. Most travel books tell you how to travel like a tourist. Although there is nothing wrong with that, as part of the Greater Than a Tourist series, this book will give you travel tips from someone who has lived at your next travel destination.

In these pages, you will discover advice that will help you throughout your stay. This book will not tell you exact addresses or store hours but instead will give you excitement and knowledge from a local that you may not find in other smaller print travel books.

Travel like a local. Slow down, stay in one place, and get to know the people and the culture. By the time you finish this book, you will be eager and prepared to travel to your next destination.

>TOURIST

TABLE OF CONTENTS

BOOK DESCRIPTION
TABLE OF CONTENTS
DEDICATION
ABOUT THE AUTHOR
HOW TO USE THIS BOOK
FROM THE PUBLISHER
OUR STORY
WELCOME TO
> TOURIST
INTRODUCTION
1. Why Visit?
2. Begin at the Visitor Center
3. Make A List of Must See Places
4. Getting to Gettysburg: Closest Airports
5. Stay in Town!
6. Rent A Car!
7. Take a Double Decker Bus!
8. Historic Place to Dine In
9. Dine With Locals
10. Have an Ice Cream at Mr. Gs
11. Things to Do with Your Kids
12. Haunted Areas to Visit
13. Plan In Advance for Gettysburg Battle Reenactment

14. Always Bring Sunscreen
15. Annual Events
16. The Most Historical Site
17. Visit Eisenhower's National Historic Site
18. Shop with the Locals
19. Best Hotels to Stay At
20. Live like a Local with AirBnB
21. Dress Like It's The 1860s
22. Camping is For Everyone!
23. Mini Golfing
24. Movie Theaters
25. Dress Appropriately with the Seasons
26. Ski Liberty
27. Durable Shoes Needed
28. Places To Visit Away from Gettysburg
29. Visit The Observatory Tower at Oak Ridge
30. Best Places to Get Pictures
31. Take An Old Fashion Photo
32. Visit The Recreational Parks!
33. Souvenirs to Bring Home
34. Books to Read Before Coming
35. Films to Watch Before Coming
36. Street Foods in Gettysburg
37. Remember these important items!
38. Out of the Ordinary Things to Do!
39. Best Horseback Riding Trails

>TOURIST

40. Be Mindful of Ticks
41. Respect The Sacred Areas
42. Accessibility Tips
43. Speak To The Locals
44. Places to Buy Groceries
45. Place to Buy Things You Might Need
46. Best Shops to Visit in Town
47. Best Apps for Gettysburg
48. Newspapers/Magazines to Look At While You're There
49. Cash or Card?
50. What Does This Place Teach You About Yourself?

TOP REASON TO BOOK THIS TRIP

50 THINGS TO KNOW ABOUT PACKING LIGHT FOR TRAVEL

Packing and Planning Tips

Travel Questions

Travel Bucket List

NOTES

DEDICATION

This book is dedicated to lives lost that day in battle at Gettysburg for without them, change for equality may not have been possible.

And to my family: Edwin, Margarita, Kimberly and Jack, who I love so dearly and will always be home in my life. You are the inspiration behind everything I do.

>TOURIST

ABOUT THE AUTHOR

Traveling back in time is a dream for not few but many people and although it may seem like you will never time travel, there are ways to visit the past including visiting places like Gettysburg, which was a dream place to live in for a person like Melody Guillen.

Melody Guillen spent over ten years living in the countryside in Gettysburg. Her parents relocated there from Reading, PA when she was three years old. Gettysburg has been the place where she spent all of her childhood and adolescent growing up, learning and dressing up as if she lived in the 19th century.

From 2nd to 8th grade, Melody was homeschooled in this area and has spent the rest of her time in the schools located in Gettysburg. While in school, she participated in many theatre productions and was heavily involved in the creative writing and German groups her school provided. She has gained many friends and family who lived in this area and still speaks to other locals in the area often.

She recalls spending time visiting museums, libraries and battlefields as she grew up and looks back on her time spent there with very fond memories. She regularly dressed up in civil war inspired clothing and participated in a few functions during her years spent living in Gettysburg.

Growing up in Gettysburg caused Melody to have a true appreciation for history and culture, which is what lead her to become a travel blogger on her website Melody Wanders.

Melody left Gettysburg, PA in 2012 but visits regularly and she will always consider it home in her heart. She will always have a deep respect for the history and culture that the town represents and she continues to read and learn about the town even from faraway.

Since leaving Melody is primarily based in Orlando, Fl where she works as a freelance writer and travel blogger. She has traveled across the globe and has learned that the best advice for travel is from locals themselves. Although she usually lives in Florida, she lives abroad for a few months out of the year and has loved becoming a local of the towns and cities she moves to.

When she is not working, she loves spending time reading, traveling on cruises to new destinations and spending time with her family including her Bichon named Jack. She is an avid reader and traveler and is always up for discovering new things.

>TOURIST
HOW TO USE THIS BOOK

The Greater Than a Tourist book series was written by someone who has lived in an area for over three months. The goal of this book is to help travelers either dream or experience different locations by providing opinions from a local. The author has made suggestions based on their own experiences. Please do your own research before traveling to the area in case the suggested places are unavailable.

Travel Advisories: As a first step in planning any trip abroad, check the Travel Advisories for your intended destination.
https://travel.state.gov/content/travel/en/traveladvisories/traveladvisories.html

FROM THE PUBLISHER

Traveling can be one of the most important parts of a person's life. The anticipation and memories that you have are some of the best. As a publisher of the Greater Than a Tourist book series, as well as the popular 50 Things to Know book series, we strive to help you learn about new places, spark your imagination, and inspire you. Wherever you are and whatever you do I wish you safe, fun, and inspiring travel.

Lisa Rusczyk Ed. D.
CZYK Publishing

\>TOURIST

OUR STORY

Traveling is a passion of the "Greater than a Tourist" series creator. Lisa studied abroad in college, and for their honeymoon Lisa and her husband toured Europe. During her travels to Malta, an older man tried to give her some advice based on his own experience living on the island since he was a young boy. She was not sure if she should talk to the stranger but was interested in his advice. When traveling to some places she was wary to talk to locals because she was afraid that they weren't being genuine. Through her travels, Lisa learned how much locals had to share with tourists. Lisa created the "Greater Than a Tourist" book series to help connect people with locals. A topic that locals are very passionate about sharing.

>TOURIST

WELCOME TO
> TOURIST

>TOURIST

INTRODUCTION

"It is for us the living, rather, to be dedicated here to the unfinished work which they who fought here have thus far so nobly advanced"

- Abraham Lincoln

Traveling back in time is all but possible in a place like Gettysburg, Pennsylvania where so many places and sights look untouched since the 1860s.

The biggest event in the Civil War happened right outside of town in Gettysburg. This event which has been known as the bloodiest battle to have happened on American soil was a much needed victory to the north Yankees to eventually win the war.

This place that is now primarily a resting site for the soldiers who fought hundreds of year is a place that was quite the turning point in the height of the Civil War and without the battle, who knows what would have happened to the United States.

Gettysburg has become a historical town, almost untouched and well respected by the thousands who visit each year and has been well preserved by the locals who have cared and loved the land. Visiting this area is a treat for all to discover and learned what really happened on those three days of battle.

>TOURIST

1. WHY VISIT?

Whether you are a lover of history or not, there are so many reasons to visit the beautiful town of Gettysburg. Here are some of the best reasons to visit!-

Gettysburg is full of stories: the battle, that many historians have said was the turning point of the civil war was right here in Gettysburg. The stories of how it all came to be lie within the fields and museums that Gettysburg offers. Where would we be now, without this place and the battle that took place here?

Lincolns Famous Speech: One of my favorite speeches of all time was said here in this little town. What may be the most famous speech in Presidential history was written as a memorial for the soldiers that died on the battlefield and as a optimistic outlook on where the country would be headed despite the loss of friends and family.

Ghosts: If you're not a lover history, you might be interested in Gettysburg for the quantity of ghost said to haunt the area. Although I never witness anything supernatural here, I do have lots of friends in the area who have. As creepy as it is to me, it is a winning point for a supernatural fan.

Beautiful All Year Round: This town is placed in the northeastern part of the United States which means that it gets every season perfectly. Not only is it beautiful all year round. It's very different that any other "historical" town because it isn't New England or the South but a whole historical town of it's own which is beautiful it's own way.

2. BEGIN AT THE VISITOR CENTER

Although Gettysburg is a small town, there is a lot of battlefields to see so going to the visitor center to map out what you'll see for the days you're there is a great start. Most people don't come to Gettysburg for very long so you want to make sure you're seeing the best and most historical places in town.

Heading to the visitor center is a great way to start because they have all the information you could ever need. It's a great way to make sure you're seeing exactly what you want to see.

>TOURIST

3. MAKE A LIST OF MUST SEE PLACES

The battlefields in Gettysburg are huge so if you're planning to be there for only a couple days, making a list of must see places is very helpful. If you prioritize what area is most important and organize your tours carefully, you'll definitely be able to see so much of Gettysburg and everything that makes it special.

4. GETTING TO GETTYSBURG: CLOSEST AIRPORTS

Gettysburg itself does have an airport called the Gettysburg Regional Airport but it carries very small airlines and if you're coming from a faraway state, I'd advise flying into a bigger airport such as:

Harrisburg International Airport MDT (36 Miles Away)
Baltimore Washington International Airport BWI (55 Miles Away)
Ronald Reagan Washington Airport DCA (78 Miles)

Washington Dulles International Airport IAD (78 Miles)

Philadelphia International Airport (118 Miles)

5. STAY IN TOWN!

Gettysburg is not known for it's trusty taxis or shuttles so I would recommend staying the in the middle of the small town because most of the battlefields and tours are walkable from the center of town. I lived in town for a couple of months while our house was getting renovated in Gettysburg and it was so easy and convenient to walk to some of my favorite places.

6. RENT A CAR!

If you're planning on staying a bit out of town, I would also recommend renting a car so you're able to see everything. Renting a car or having your own car there really makes a difference because you're able to have your own tour and take time going to the places you really wanted to see.

>TOURIST

The battlefields are huge and all around and renting a car to see it all makes it easier on yourself. I lived right next to the battlefields and my family and I often took afternoon drives to see the sunsets across the fields which was always special.

7. TAKE A DOUBLE DECKER BUS!

If you are planning on staying outside of town and/or not renting a car, then I would say the best option to see it all is to take a double decker bus! They're super cool and fun especially if you come with a family. You're able to see a lot of historical places while not getting to exhausted from walking.

8. HISTORIC PLACE TO DINE IN

Gettysburg is an old town and with that comes places to eat that have been around for awhile. Here is an older more historic place to eat at if you want something a little more special.

Dobbin House Tavern

They serve the best French onion soup I've ever had and the best part about it is all the history that surrounds you while you eat. This tavern was used as a notable hospital during and after the Battle of Gettysburg.

9. DINE WITH LOCALS

Locals don't often visit the finest restaurants in town but instead enjoy a great meal with friends in a more causal place.

Lincoln Diner: This place is a true local hang out. It's been in the middle of Gettysburg for over sixty years and is open 24/7. The place is a classic diner setting with folks who have been dining here for decades.

Appalachian Brewery: A company of breweries in town that serve lots of unique and specialty drinks and beers along with really great food.

Friendly's: While I know this is a chain restaurant but it's a place I've been eating at since I was 3 years old. Many of the employees have been there for years and always remember the locals which is sweet. They serve amazing sundaes that you have to try while you're in town no matter the weather.

Tommy's Pizza: Another local hang out is this pizzeria that is in town and has some of the most amazing pizzas you'll ever try.

10. HAVE AN ICE CREAM AT MR. GS

When my sister was in middle school, she would walk here almost everyday to get a scoop of the best ice cream in town. This is a very popular spot in the summer that sometimes has lines out the door. If you're looking for some classic made ice cream, this is the place for you.

11. THINGS TO DO WITH YOUR KIDS

I loved growing up and being homeschooled in Gettysburg because of the history it held and all the interesting places to visit. If you're coming here with your kids and you're worried about what to do with them, don't be because there are so many cool places to visit that are perfect for young children.

Explore and More

I use to beg my mom to take me here for years. It's an interactive museum designed for kids to explore scientific things, dress up as 1800s people, and design there own stuff. It's such a cool place and I miss visiting it even now.

Gettysburg Library

This library is a treat I think for all ages but as a young child, I loved coming here with my mom almost everyday. The ladies who work in the kids department are super sweet and some of them have been working there for years. They do some really great story times and activities so check out there

>TOURIST

website for more details. The building used for the library is also very old and historical itself which is a bonus.

Local Recreational Parks

This town is filled with lots of great parks and nature and it is a shame to miss it. They are tons of places and parks to take you're kids to release some energy and have fun!

12. HAUNTED AREAS TO VISIT

Gettysburg is famous for it's ghosts and ghost tours that are offered in town at night. There are many places to visit if you're into haunted and creepy adventures, and here are some of my favorites.

Sashes Covered Bridge

The Grove

Devils Den

Jennie Wade's House: The home of the only civilian killed

Servant's Old Thyme

Many of these places can be seen all in one night if you pick a good long ghost tour. Many of the ghost tours can also be kid friendly. These areas are perfect for a chilly October afternoon if you're in the mood to see some haunted unrested souls.

13. PLAN IN ADVANCE FOR GETTYSBURG BATTLE REENACTMENT

Gettysburg's busiest time is July 1st-4th because of it is the anniversary of the Battle of Gettysburg. People from all over the word come, dress up and join in on so many festivities that the town has. As exciting as it can be, the town is very small and is absolutely packed for the majority of these four days.

I would advise to plan as much as you can in advance for these dates. Book your hotel or Airbnb way ahead of schedule because Gettysburg in terms

>TOURIST

of size is very small with a population of nearly 8,000 people and hotel space is always limited.

Book restaurants, space and events also way ahead of time to avoid not being able to enter because of over crowding. As busy as this time is, it's always a treat to see thousands of people come, dress up and join in on the reenactment of this famous battle.

14. ALWAYS BRING SUNSCREEN

The battlefields are large and grand but also don't have tons of shade. In the summer Gettysburg gets really hot and sunny so I advise bringing lots of sunscreen to protect from the sun's rays. Even in the off seasons, I'd still recommend bringing sunscreen because of how open the fields are and the lack of trees and shade in the battlefields.

15. ANNUAL EVENTS

Although Gettysburg is famous for the Battle of Gettysburg that took place in the summer, there are tons of events that happen throughout the year that are also tons of fun and historical.

May: Apple Blossom Festival
June: Gettysburg Festival
July: Annual Civil War Reenactment
August: Gettysburg Bluegrass Festival
September: Gettysburg Wine and Music Festival
October: National Apple Harvest
November: Gettysburg Address Anniversary
December: Holidays in Gettysburg (My favorite time of the year in Gettysburg!)

16. THE MOST HISTORICAL SITE

"Four score and seven years ago.." The beginning of what would be the most popular speech ever written by a president was first heard in this little town of Gettysburg. The speech that has been uttered millions of times in schools across the nation was first said in an area where many of the soldiers bodies rested.

President Abraham Lincoln visited the town and payed his respects a few months after the battle because of how long it took for the bodies to finally be rested and the smell in the air calm down. The

>TOURIST

speech is one of my favorites and the fact that it was told in a place I called home makes it even better.

This speech has continued to inspire people all over the world that among the roughest time, we can get back up and move forward stronger than before. I make it a point to visit the Lincoln Gettysburg Address Memorial, any chance I get so that I can stand where he once stood and feel as moved and inspired as he did.

17. VISIT EISENHOWER'S NATIONAL HISTORIC SITE

During and after being the nations's 34th president of the United States, Dwight D. Eisenhower settle on the outskirts of Gettysburg. He purchased the home with his wife in 1950 and finally lived there officially after they left the White House in 1961.

This place is a really interesting place to see that many people might don't know is in the area of Gettysburg. I used to live really close to this home and would drive by and wondered what Eisenhower would spend his days doing in the countryside of Pennsylvania.

They have tours of the home now that you can take and get an insiders look on how he lived his life here in Gettysburg.

18. SHOP WITH THE LOCALS

Many of the locals, including myself have spent numerous amount of hours shopping in the outlets that are right outside of the downtown area of Gettysburg. The outlets have tons and tons of great shops and restaurants to visit if you're in the mood for more locals things.

They feature shops like Bath and Body Works, Adidas, American Eagle and much more! Because it is a an outlet, the clothes and items in store are way cheaper than regular shops. Many of the tourist don't know too much about this area so other than the summer, the shops are rarely busy.

>TOURIST

19. BEST HOTELS TO STAY AT

Although I lived in this town for more a decade, I did spend some times in the hotels during a renovation of my house. There are a few number of hotels to visit and stay at and while some of them are more historic than others these are my favorites ranked

1. Wyndham Gettysburg: The best out of the bunch as it's only a few years old and I remember them building it when I was younger. It's super clean and the staff is great. Very close to a movie theatre and some restaurants. However it's a few miles away from the heart of the town.

2. Courtyard by Marriott: Another good option right next to the Wyndham is this hotel which is also really nice and clean. But again is a bit away from town.

3. Gettysburg Hotel: One of the oldest hotels that hosted Abraham Lincoln and where it is said he finished up writing the famous Gettysburg Address. Although it is super famous, it's also very old but has that classic charm to it that will be appealing to historians of all kind.

20. LIVE LIKE A LOCAL WITH AIRBNB

Renting an apartment or a house for the time you're there is also a great option when staying in Gettysburg. There are tons of apartments and town houses that are in the center of the town you can stay at to get that true local feel. The places that are directly in town are truly the best and I would tell you to take the opportunity to live in some of Gettysburg's oldest buildings in town to feel like you're truly back in time.

21. DRESS LIKE IT'S THE 1860S

When I was young I loved dressing up like I was back in time and the people living in this town encouraged it. Although it might be weird to some people, it was magical to walk around the town and catch a glimpse of a man or women who looked like they came right out of a historical book.

If you have the chance to make your own or order a dress, I say go for it! Especially for the reenactment in July, there are tons of parties and events where they want you to go all in on the props.

22. CAMPING IS FOR EVERYONE!

If you're a fan of the outdoors and camping, I would highly recommend staying at one of the many campsites in Gettysburg. Doing this is a way to have fun with the whole family and also meet some new friends.

I often went camping with my family in these areas and I always had a blast. I also lived by a campsite for some time and could always hear the cheers of fun being had.

23. MINI GOLFING

A fun activity to do with your family or even a spouse or partner that you're with is to go mini golfing. There are a couple really cool mini golfing areas you can visit with friends and family. Locals go mini golfing a lot with family, friends and even go with dates for a cute romantic evening.

I highly recommend checking this out if you're in the mood for some fun out of the ordinary activities.

24. MOVIE THEATERS

Although the population of Gettysburg is small, the town has more than enough theaters for everyone. One of my favorite things is heading to the movies to see something new especially on Tuesdays because many of the regular theaters have discounts and tickets for less than $5 dollars.

Majestic Theatre: Historical space that has been there for decades. It has lots of retro charm and often offers live theatre, music and shows classic films. You'll probably won't find the latest blockbuster films here but they often have indie films showing here which can be cool.

Gateway Theatre: Probably my favorite out of the bunch. It has 8 screens and usually offers a great discount on Tuesdays. The film rooms are very spacious and offer lots of comfortable seating.

>TOURIST

Frank Theaters Gettysburg Village Stadium 10: My least favorite out of the group but it does offer more film rooms which often means that it has more film options.

25. DRESS APPROPRIATELY WITH THE SEASONS

Gettysburg is in Pennsylvania which is a northeastern state. This means that the state has every single season and the weather is always true to the season it's in.

If it's winter, it will be cold and maybe some snow. Make sure you bring a good coat, hat and hand mittens.

If it's spring, expect lukewarm weather and flowers in bloom. Make sure you bring layers of clothing because the weather can go from cold mornings to warm afternoons back to cold.

If it's autumn, it'll most likely be cool crisp weather and sunny skies. Bring plenty of layers and warm sweaters.

If it's summer, it will probably be very warm and hot on most days. Bring light summer clothing as well as a rain jacket for the occasional rainy days.

26. SKI LIBERTY

Eight miles away from Gettysburg lies this little oasis for people who love all things ski and snow! Some people don't know about this cool ski resort that resides close to Gettysburg. If you're a big fan of ski resorts and snow while you're in the area, I would definitely check this place out.

I often went in the winter to go snow tubing and drink some hot chocolate during the winter months and I loved it. It was so fun to go with family and friends and enjoy the season of winter by the slopes.

27. DURABLE SHOES NEEDED

Like I've mentioned before, although the town of Gettysburg is small, the actual battlefields are huge so you need to remember to bring your best durable shoes. The shoes have to be good for walking and going through muddy areas. You never know what

>TOURIST

you might encounter on the battlefields whether it might be mud, dry patches, rocks and having good shoes will helps a lot.

28. PLACES TO VISIT AWAY FROM GETTYSBURG

Although the quaint town of Gettysburg is always a treat, taking a day away can also be fun. Here are some of my favorite places to visit that aren't too far and have tons of things to do.

Hanover (14 Miles) : A town filled with tons of shops, restaurants and activities for everyone. I came here a lot when I was young to visit the mall and eat out.

Camp Hill (35 Miles): A borough only 3 miles away from Harrisburg that contains an even bigger mall and more activities to do.

Washington D.C (86 Miles): The one and only capital of the United States is a little more than an hour and a half away from Gettysburg and has museums and monuments galore.

29. VISIT THE OBSERVATORY TOWER AT OAK RIDGE

This resides very close to my childhood home and I biked here sometimes with my dad. The tower is super cool and you are able to see so much of the battlefields from up there. I would highly recommend visiting this not so known place where you'll really be able to get a scope of the whole area.

30. BEST PLACES TO GET PICTURES

As a photography lover myself, there are some incredible spots to take pictures here in Gettysburg especially at sunset/sunrise time.

Eternal Light Peace Memorial
Observatory Tower
Confederate Avenue
Little Ground Top
Devils Den
Wheat Field Road
Virginia Memorial
Pennsylvania Memorial
National Cemetery

>TOURIST

31. TAKE AN OLD FASHION PHOTO

Inside town, there are tons of great places that offer taking photos of you and your friends and family in 1860 clothing that will make you look like you're back in the past. A neighbor of ours did this and it was really cool to see how it was done and how good the picture looks when it's finished. This is a great souvenir to take back home with you to remember you're unforgettable trip.

32. VISIT THE RECREATIONAL PARKS!

As I've previously mentioned, visiting the parks can be really fun and beautiful. There is a lot of nature in Gettysburg because nearly everything is a landmark so they can't build much on it. Because of this, there are loads of normal park areas that aren't necessarily battlefields. I used to come here as a kid and I still visit even though I've grown up.

These are great places to bring your dog if he's along for the trip or your kids like I mentioned in a tip before. The recreational park can be quite pretty and very relaxing to visit if you're in the mood for a nature walk and some peace and quiet.

33. SOUVENIRS TO BRING HOME

I lived in Gettysburg for a long time and by living here I've seen all the souvenirs from the most basic to the most pointless of gifts. I always love a good souvenir and gift to bring back home to family and friends so here are a couple of good souvenirs to buy if you're in town.

T - Shirts and Hoodies: My favorite form of souvenir and gift to buy from anywhere because it's the most likely to be used.

Key Chains: These are actually really great gifts to get friends and I always enjoy a cute keychain for a set of boring keys.

Coffee Mugs or Tumblrs: Another great practical gift or souvenir to get because you'll actually use it and is a great story to tell people when they visit and use it.

Historical Book: Because Gettysburg is so historical, this is a good souvenir to have for your bookshelf or coffee table.

34. BOOKS TO READ BEFORE COMING

Even though I haven't read some of these myself, I have worked at a bookstore for a long time and these have been some of the most popular books to read about Gettysburg. Reading about a place before you go as always been my favorite thing to do because it gets you excited to go and makes the places come to life which is really cool.

Gettysburg: The Last Invasion - Allen C. Guelzo

The Killer Angels - Michael Shaara

Gettysburg - Stephen W Sears

Gone With The Wind - Margaret Mitchell: Although the story never takes place in Gettysburg, the time period is around the same and they mention Gettysburg in the novel.

35. FILMS TO WATCH BEFORE COMING

Another great thing to do before coming is watching some films to get you excited about visiting a new place. Gettysburg obviously is very historical but it's actually been the setting to many films you might not have known about. Here are some of my favorites that either are about the town or were filmed there.

Gettysburg (1993 Film): A war film about the biggest event in the Civil War.

Abraham Lincoln: Vampire Hunter (2012 Film): A unique spin on the famous president. The perfect film for an adventure or fantasy film lover that mentions historic moments.

Gone With The Wind (1939 Film): The classic epic historic romance that never does show Gettysburg but mentions the events. It also is set in that time period and what things were like in the south during the Civil War.

>TOURIST

Lincoln (2012 Film): Although the events of the film are after Gettysburg it's still within the time period and it's a really great film.

Remember the Titans (2000 Film): A biographical sport film about the true story of of a newly appointed African-American coach and his high school team on their first season as a racially integrated unit. One of the most memorable scenes was filmed in Gettysburg which I find really fascinating.

36. STREET FOODS IN GETTYSBURG

While Gettysburg may not necessarily have street food like New York City, they do have some hidden gems and one of my favorites in this Mexican restaurant that serves some of the best food I've ever had called Tania's Mexican Restaurant. Another place to visit for some Chinese food is Li's Buffet which is a local favorite. Be sure to visit these places and you'll thank me later!

37. REMEMBER THESE IMPORTANT ITEMS!

Although I've mentioned sunscreen and good shoes, there are a couple other things you should bring with you to Gettysburg.

A good camera: There are so many beautiful places to capture at all times in this little town.

Clothes that you don't mind getting dirty

Rain Jacket and Umbrella: If it rains, there isn't much place to hide from the water

Guide Book: So you don't always have to rely on your tour guide

Long Pants: Be aware of poisonous plants in some more rural areas

38. OUT OF THE ORDINARY THINGS TO DO!

Gettysburg isn't always just battlefields and museums, there is actually tons to see and do here that you might not do at home. I find this place to be beautiful and getting involved in some local activity can make your trip all the more special.

>TOURIST

Go Horseback Riding!: There are a ton of places to visit and ride at and it's something I used to do as a kid and loved. The town is surrounded by lots of hidden woods and this is a great way to see the land and have some fun!

Deer Hunting: Although this might not be for everyone, this is a fairly popular thing to do in Gettysburg. If you're a hunter yourself this might be the perfect thing to do in such a memorable place like this.

39. BEST HORSEBACK RIDING TRAILS

There are so many great places to visit and horseback ride on and here are some of the best trails to go on if you're in the mood for a little adventure!

Hickory Hollow Horse Farm

Confederate Trails of Gettysburg

National Riding Stables

40. BE MINDFUL OF TICKS

Gettysburg is very rural and because of this, there is a lot of wild life like deers and most of all ticks. If you're in the area where there may be ticks, be sure to take some precautions to be safe.

There are clothes you can buy that have built in tick repellent you can buy. Another good thing to wear is light colored clothing. Also make sure you tuck your pants into your socks.

There are tons of sprays, ointments and clothes you can wear to protect yourself and ask locals for even more tips on how to be safe depending on the time of year you go. Check you and your family for ticks regularly.

41. RESPECT THE SACRED AREAS

Everyone knows that thousands of soldiers died here in Gettysburg so this town has become sort of a quiet and hallowed place. Many locals have great respect for the cemeteries and battlefields because of what it entails and if you're visiting you should be

>TOURIST

mindful of that. Respect the space, monuments and the areas of where these soldiers sacrificed so much.

42. ACCESSIBILITY TIPS

The park has many paved roads (about 25 miles) that are open for touring with a private vehicle. All tour guides are meant to be mobility friendly and accessible but beware for uneven paths and weather conditions that may change this.

Mobility Access: You can tour the battlefields and grounds with your own vehicle. There are a couple of private touring companies that have bus tours and are very mobility friendly that you can research and book with.

Hearing Impairments: When you visit the Visitor Center, I recommend getting one of the free map and tour guide to use and read. Many of the tours include text and visual illustrations that are throughout the battlefields

Visual Impairments: The best thing I would recommend is hiring a licensed battlefield guide at the

Visitor Center which will provide a two hour guide. There are various audio stations throughout the battlefields and almost all the monuments and cannon are touchable. There is also lots of brail across the town and fields.

43. SPEAK TO THE LOCALS

As a local myself, I love meeting new people from all over the world so when the busy summer season hits Gettysburg, I always make it a point to try and meet as many people as possible. Don't be afraid to talk to the locals and ask them questions in person because many of them have been living here for years. By doing this, you might have a great conversation and learn something new.

44. PLACES TO BUY GROCERIES

Being in town can get really crowded and finding a place to simply buy some water and snacks is hard but I have a couple of great places to buy some groceries if you're in Gettysburg.

>TOURIST

Giant: Although it's not the only grocery store in town, it does have the most products at the best price which is always great.

Kennie's Market: A regular grocery store that does tend to get busy during the high season of Gettysburg but is right in the middle of town and within walking distance of many downtown hotels.

7 Eleven: I used to come here as a kid and get slurpees during the summer and donuts during the winter. Even though it's small, it's in town which makes it convenient for small things like snacks.

45. PLACE TO BUY THINGS YOU MIGHT NEED

Walmart is a little out of the ways but the best place to buy anything you may have forgotten or need for the trip. If you need batteries, sleeping bags or a camera, this is the best store in town. It's about a mile away from downtown Gettysburg but is worth it in my opinion.

46. BEST SHOPS TO VISIT IN TOWN

Sweet! THE Candy Store in Gettysburg PA! This shops is local and tourist treat for all ages to visit. This store has all kinds of old and new candies to try that you wouldn't see in a regular store.

The Crystal Wand: The metaphysical store for spiritualist from all around that offers crystals, books and more. Come in and breathe in the calm and serenity that this shop has to offer,

The Antique Center of Gettysburg: There are many antique stores in town but this one has always been my favorite. There are so many interesting trinkets, photos and more in this place that date back all the way to before the civil war. I always managed to find something cool to purchase here in a store like this.

47. BEST APPS FOR GETTYSBURG

Although Gettysburg is an old town, it has moved up with the times and there are lots of great apps to use for your trip.

>TOURIST

Gettysburg Battle App (Available for Android and iPhone, free): This GPS enabled app provides a wonderful overview of the battle with a chronology, list of facts, an interactive map to make your trip special.

Historic Gettysburg Walking Tour (Available for Android and iPhone, free): This app focusses more on downtown Gettysburg instead of the battlefields but offers a pretty good guide for this people interested in walking down the town streets after going to the battlefields.

Gettysburg 150 Facts about The 150th (Available for iPad, $1.99): This app easily explains in a fun and interactive way about the most important facts about the battle. Also offers a look into a typical day in the life of an average Civil War solider.

48. NEWSPAPERS/MAGAZINES TO LOOK AT WHILE YOU'RE THERE

Another way to get more facts about the town is by checking out the local magazines and newspaper.

Gettysburg Magazine: Established in 1989, this magazine publishes engaging articles and work about the battles and concerns of Gettysburg. Great readings for historical, field and personal essays if you're interested in any of these categories surrounding Gettysburg.

Gettysburg Times: Founded in 1904, is a daily newspaper that talks about the news of modern to historical times in the town of Gettysburg.

49. CASH OR CARD?

In a historical place such as this, you may be wondering if you should bring some cash in case the places you visit don't take card. I would advise to not worry about it too much because theres a ton of banks to take money out. However, if you're headed to the battlefields for the whole day, I recommend taking

>TOURIST

some cash out for food and water stands that may be out.

50. WHAT DOES THIS PLACE TEACH YOU ABOUT YOURSELF?

Gettysburg, my first home town and a place I always look at with fond memories and love. Although it may not be your hometown, it's where you are able to learn so much of our past and in turn learn how to be better for the future.

In this place that was once so divided, you're able to look back on the past with other people and enjoy the area for what is was: A great battlefield, a final resting place for the soldiers who died here and a realization that we can grow and become a nation united.

Abraham Lincoln once said "It is rather for us to be here dedicated to the great task remaining before us—that from these honored dead we take increased devotion to that cause for which they here gave the last full measure of devotion—that we here highly resolve that these dead shall not have died in vain—

that this nation, under God, shall have a new birth of freedom, and that government of the people, by the people, for the people, shall not perish from the earth."

>TOURIST

TOP REASON TO BOOK THIS TRIP

History: Nearly every inch of Gettysburg can still be consider a battlefield and a place that has been preserve for history lovers of all kinds to visit. A place that draws you in with adventure and stories of men who fought bravely for things they so passionately believed in.

Ghosts: If you're a fan of haunted places, this is the town for you. With so many stories of souls unrested that have come to haunt the grounds, you will have tons to see and discover if you love a good creepy tales that can be read and told all across town.

Countryside: As a lover of the countryside myself, Gettysburg is emerged in the beauty of the northeastern woods and fields. This is a place where you are able to go hiking, horseback riding, and deer hunting. Gettysburg is a true oasis for the outdoor adventurer and for anyone you loves a beautiful view.

>TOURIST

BONUS BOOK

50 THINGS TO KNOW ABOUT PACKING LIGHT FOR TRAVEL

PACK THE RIGHT WAY EVERY TIME

AUTHOR: MANIDIPA BHATTACHARYYA

First Published in 2015 by Dr. Lisa Rusczyk. Copyright 2015. All Rights Reserved. No part of this publication may be reproduced, including scanning and photocopying, or distributed in any form or by any means, electronic or mechanical, or stored in a database or retrieval system without prior written permission from the publisher.

Disclaimer: The publisher has put forth an effort in preparing and arranging this book. The information provided herein by the author is provided "as is". Use this information at your own risk. The publisher is not a licensed doctor. Consult your doctor before engaging in any medical activities. The publisher and author disclaim any liabilities for any loss of profit or commercial or personal damages resulting from the information contained in this book.

Edited by Melanie Howthorne

ABOUT THE AUTHOR

Manidipa Bhattacharyya is a creative writer and editor, with an education in English literature and Linguistics. After working in the IT industry for seven long years she decided to call it quits and follow her heart instead. Manidipa has been ghost writing, editing, proof reading and doing secondary research services for many story tellers and article writers for about three years. She stays in Kolkata, India with her husband and a busy two year old. In her own time Manidipa enjoys travelling, photography and writing flash fiction.

Manidipa believes in travelling light and never carries anything that she couldn't haul herself on a trip. However, travelling with her child changed the scenario. She seemed to carry the entire world with her for the baby on the first two trips. But good sense prevailed and she is again working her way to becoming a light traveler, this time with a kid.

\>TOURIST

INTRODUCTION

*He who would travel happily
must travel light.*

-Antoine de Saint-Exupéry

Travel takes you to different places from seas and mountains to deserts and much more. In your travels you get to interact with different people and their cultures. You will, however, enjoy the sights and interact positively with these new people even more, if you are travelling light.

When you travel light your mind can be free from worry about your belongings. You do not have to spend precious vacation time waiting for your luggage to arrive after a long flight. There is be no chance of your bags going missing and the best part is that you need not pay a fee for checked baggage.

People who have mastered this art of packing light will root for you to take only one carry-on, wherever you go. However, many people can find it really hard to pack light. More so if you are travelling with children. Differentiating between "must have" and "just in case" items is the starting point. There will be ample shopping avenues at your destination which are just waiting to be explored.

This book will show you 'packing' in a new 'light' – pun intended – and help you to embrace light packing practices for all of your future travels.

Off to packing!

DEDICATION

I dedicate this book to all the travel buffs that I know, who have given me great insights into the contents of their backpacks.

THE RIGHT TRAVEL GEAR

1. CHOOSE YOUR TRAVEL GEAR CAREFULLY

While selecting your travel gear, pick items that are light weight, durable and most importantly, easy to carry. There are cases with wheels so you can drag them along – these are usually on the heavy side because of the trolley. Alternatively a backpack that you can carry comfortably on your back, or even a duffel bag that you can carry easily by hand or sling across your body are also great options. Whatever you choose, one thing to keep in mind is that the luggage itself should not weigh a ton, this will give you the flexibility to bring along one extra pair of shoes if you so desire.

>TOURIST

2. CARRY THE MINIMUM NUMBER OF BAGS

Selecting light weight luggage is not everything. You need to restrict the number of bags you carry as well. One carry-on size bag is ideal for light travel. Most carriers allow one cabin baggage plus one purse, handbag or camera bag as long as it slides under the seat in front. So technically, you can carry two items of luggage without checking them in.

3. PACK ONE EXTRA BAG

Always pack one extra empty bag along with your essential items. This could be a very light weight duffel bag or even a sturdy tote bag which takes up minimal space. In the event that you end up buying a lot of souvenirs, you already have a handy bag to stuff all that into and do not have to spend time hunting for an appropriate bag.

I'm very strict with my packing and have everything in its right place. I never change a rule. I hardly use anything in the hotel room. I wheel my own wardrobe in and that's it.

Charlie Watts

CLOTHES & ACCESSORIES

4. PLAN AHEAD

Figure out in advance what you plan to do on your trip. That will help you to pick that one dress you need for the occasion. If you are going to attend a wedding then you have to carry formal wear. If not, you can ditch the gown for something lighter that will be comfortable during long walks or on the beach.

5. WEAR THAT JACKET

Remember that wearing items will not add extra luggage for your air travel. So wear that bulky jacket that you plan to carry for your trip. This saves space and can also help keep you warm during the chilly flight.

6. MIX AND MATCH

Carry clothes that can be interchangeably used to reinvent your look. Find one top that goes well with a couple of pairs of pants or skirts. Use tops, shirts and jackets wisely along with other accessories like a scarf or a stole to create a new look.

>TOURIST

7. CHOOSE YOUR FABRIC WISELY

Stuffing clothes in cramped bags definitely takes its toll which results in wrinkles. It is best to carry wrinkle free, synthetic clothes or merino tops. This will eliminate the need for that small iron you usually bring along.

8. DITCH CLOTHES PACK UNDERWEAR

Pack more underwear and socks. These are the things that will give you a fresh feel even if you do not get a chance to wear fresh clothes. Moreover these are easy to wash and can be dried inside the hotel room itself.

9. CHOOSE DARK OVER LIGHT

While picking your clothes choose dark coloured ones. They are easy to colour coordinate and can last longer before needing a wash. Accidental food spills and dirt from the road are less visible on darker clothes.

10. WEAR YOUR JEANS

Take only one pair of Jeans with you, which you should wear on the flight. Remember to pick a pair that can be worn for sightseeing trips and is equally eloquent for dinner. You can add variety by adding light weight cargoes and chinos.

11. CARRY SMART ACCESSORIES

The right accessory can give you a fresh look even with the same old dress. An intelligent neck-piece, a couple of bright scarves, stoles or a sarong can be used in a number of ways to add variety to your clothing. These light weight beauties can double up as a nursing cover, a light blanket, beach wear, a modesty cover for visiting places of worship, and also makes for an enthralling game of peek-a-boo.

12. LEARN TO FOLD YOUR GARMENTS

Seasoned travellers all swear by rolling their clothes for compact and wrinkle free packing. Bundle packing, where you roll the clothes around a central object as if tying it up, is also a popular method of compact and wrinkle free packing. Stacking folded clothes one on top of another is a big no-no as it makes creases extreme and they are difficult to get rid of without ironing.

>TOURIST

13. WASH YOUR DIRTY LAUNDRY

One of the ways to avoid carrying loads of clothes is to wash the clothes you carry. At some places you might get to use the laundry services or a Laundromat but if you are in a pinch, best solution is to wash them yourself. If that is the plan then carrying quick drying clothes is highly recommended, which most often also happen to be the wrinkle free variety.

14. LEAVE THOSE TOWELS BEHIND

Regular towels take up a lot of space, are heavy and take ages to dry out. If you are staying at hotels they will provide you with towels anyway. If you are travelling to a remote place, where the availability of towels look doubtful, carry a light weight travel towel of viscose material to do the job.

15. USE A COMPRESSION BAG

Compression bags are getting lots of recommendation now days from regular travellers. These are useful for saving space in your luggage when you have to pack bulky dresses. While packing for the return trip, get help from the hotel staff to arrange a vacuum cleaner.

FOOTWEAR

16. PUT ON YOUR HIKING BOOTS

If you have plans to go hiking or trekking during your trip, you will need those bulky hiking boots. The best way to carry them is to wear them on flight to save space and luggage weight. You can remove the boots once inside and be comfortable in your socks.

17. PICKING THE RIGHT SHOES

Shoes are often the bulkiest items, along with being the dainty if you are a female. They need care and take up a lot of space in your luggage. It is advisable therefore to pick shoes very carefully. If you plan to do a lot of walking and site seeing, then wearing a pair of comfortable walking shoes are a must. For more formal occasions you can carry durable, light weight flats which will not take up much space.

18. STUFF SHOES

If you happen to pack a pair of shoes, ensure you utilize their hollow insides. Tuck small items like rolled up socks or belts to save space. They will also be easy to find.

>TOURIST

TOILETRIES

19. STASHING TOILETRIES

Carry only absolute necessities. Airline rules dictate that for one carry-on bag, liquids and gels must be in 3.4 ounce (100ml) bottles or less, and must be packed in a one quart zip-lock bag. If you are planning to stay in a hotel, the basic things will be provided for you. It's best is to buy the rest from the local market at your destination.

20. TAKE ALONG TAMPONS

Tampons are a hard to find item in a lot of countries. Figure out how many you need and pack accordingly. For longer stays you can buy them online and have them delivered to where you are staying.

21. GET PAMPERED BEFORE YOU TRAVEL

Some avid travellers suggest getting a pedicure and manicure just the day before travelling. This not only gives you a well kept look, you also save the trouble of packing nail polish. Remember, every little bit of weight reduced adds up.

ELECTRONICS

22. LUGGING ALONG ELECTRONICS

Electronics have a large role to play in our lives today. Most of us cannot imagine our lives away from our phones, laptops or tablets. However while travelling, one must consider the amount of weight these electronics add to our luggage. Thankfully smart phones come along with all the essentials tools like a camera, email access, picture editing tools and more. They are smart to the point of eliminating the need to carry multiple gadgets. Choose a smart phone that suits all your requirements and travel with the world in your palms or pocket.

23. REDUCE THE NUMBER OF CHARGERS

If you do travel with multiple electronic devices, you will have to bear the additional burden of carrying all their chargers too. Check if a single charger can be used for multiple devices. You might also consider investing in a pocket charger. These small devices support multiple devices while keeping you charged on the go.

>TOURIST

24. TRAVEL FRIENDLY APPS

Along with smart phones come numerous apps, which are immensely helpful in our travels. You name it and you have an app for it at hand – take pictures, sharing with friends and family, torch to light dark roads, maps, checking flight/train times, find hotels and many other things. Use these smart alternatives to traditional items like books to eliminate weight and save space.

I get ideas about what's essential when packing my suitcase.

-Diane von Furstenberg

TRAVELLING WITH KIDS

25. BRING ALONG THE STROLLER

Kids might enjoy walking for a while but they soon tire out and a stroller is the just the right thing for them to rest in while you continue your tour. Strollers also double duty as a luggage carrier and shopping bag holder. Remember to pick a light weight, easy to handle brand of stroller. Better yet, find out in advance if you can rent a stroller at your destination.

26. BRING ONLY ENOUGH DIAPERS FOR YOUR TRIP

Diapers take up a lot of space and add to the weight of your luggage. Therefore it is advisable to carry just enough diapers to last through the trip and a few for afterwards, till you buy fresh stock at your destination. Unless of course you are travelling to a really remote area, in which case you have no choice but to carry the load. Otherwise diapers are something you will find pretty easily.

27. TAKE ONLY A COUPLE OF TOYS

Children are easily attracted by new things in their environment. While travelling they will find numerous 'new' objects to scrutinize and play with. Packing just one favorite toy is enough, or if there is no favorite toy leave out all of them in favor of stories or imaginary games.

28. CARRY KID FRIENDLY SNACKS

Create a small snack counter in your bag to store away quick bites for those sudden hunger pangs. Depending on the child's age this could include chocolates, raisins, dry fruits, granola bars or biscuits. Also keep a bottle of water handy for your little one.

>TOURIST

These things do not add much weight and can be adjusted in a handbag or knapsack.

29. GAMES TO CARRY

Create some travel specific, imaginary games if you have slightly grown up children, like spot the attractions. Keep a coloring book and colors handy for in-flight or hotel time. Apps on your smart phone can keep the children engaged with cartoons and story books. Older children are often entertained by games available on phones or tablets. This cuts the weight of luggage down while keeping the kids entertained.

30. LET THE KIDS CARRY THEIR LOAD

A good thing is to start early sharing of responsibilities. Let your child pick a bag of his or her choice and pack it themselves. Keep tabs on what they are stuffing in their bags by asking if they will be using that item on the trip. It could start out being just an entertainment bag initially but with growing years they will learn to sort the useful from the superfluous. Children as little as four can maneuver a small trolley suitcase like a pro- their experience in pull along toys credit. If you are worried that you may be pulling it for them, you may want to start with a backpack.

31. DECIDE ON LOCATION FOR CHILDREN TO SLEEP

While on a trip you might not always get a crib at your destination, and carrying one will make life all the more difficult. Instead call ahead to see if there are any cribs or roll out beds for children. You may even put blankets on the floor. Weave them a story about camping and they will gladly sleep without any trouble.

32. GET BABY PRODUCTS DELIVERED AT YOUR DESTINATION

If you are absolutely paranoid about not getting your favourite variety of diaper or brand of baby food, check out online stores like amazon.com for services in your destination city. You can buy things online ahead of your travel and get them delivered to your hotel upon arrival.

33. FEEDING NEEDS OF YOUR INFANTS

If you are travelling with a breastfed infant, you save the trouble of carrying bottles and bottle sanitization kits. For special food, or medications, you may need to call ahead to make sure you have a refrigerator where you are staying.

34. FEEDING NEEDS OF YOUR TODDLER

With the progression from infancy to toddler, their dietary requirements too evolve. You will have to pack some snacks for travelling time. Fresh fruits and vegetables can be purchased at your destination. Most of the cities you travel to in whichever part of the world, will have baby food products and formulas, available at the local drug-store or the supermarket.

35. PICKING CLOTHES FOR YOUR BABY

Contrary to popular belief, babies can do without many changes of clothes. At the most pack 2 outfits per day. Pack mix and match type clothes for your little one as well. Pick things which are comfortable to wear and quick to dry.

36. SELECTING SHOES FOR YOUR BABY

Like outfits, kids can make do with two pairs of comfortable shoes. If you can get some water resistant shoes it will be best. To expedite drying wet shoes, you can stuff newspaper in them then wrap them with newspaper and leave them to dry overnight.

37. KEEP ONE CHANGE OF CLOTHES HANDY

Travelling with kids can be tricky. Keep a change of clothes for the kids and mum handy in your purse or tote bag. This takes a bit of space in your hand luggage but comes extremely handy in case there are any accidents or spills.

38. LEAVE BEHIND BABY ACCESSORIES

Baby accessories like their bed, bath tub, car seat, crib etc. should be left at home. Many hotels provide a crib on request, while car seats can be borrowed from friends or rented. Babies can be given a bath in the hotel sink or even in the adult bath tub with a little bit of water. If you bring a few bath toys, they can be used in the bath, pool, and out of water. They can also be sanitized easily in the sink.

39. CARRY A SMALL LOAD OF PLASTIC BAGS

With children around there are chances of a number of soiled clothes and diapers. These plastic bags help to sort the dirt from the clean inside your big bag.

These are very light weight and come in handy to other carry stuff as well at times.

PACK WITH A PURPOSE

40. PACKING FOR BUSINESS TRIPS

One neutral-colored suit should suffice. It can be paired with different shirts, ties and accessories for different occasions. One pair of black suit pants could be worn with a matching jacket for the office or with a snazzy top for dinner.

41. PACKING FOR A CRUISE

Most cruises have formal dinners, and that formal dress usually takes up a lot of space. However you might find a tuxedo to rent. For women, a short black dress with multiple accessory options will do the trick.

42. PACKING FOR A LONG TRIP OVER DIFFERENT CLIMATES

The secret packing mantra for travel over multiple climates is layering. Layering traps air around your body creating insulation against the cold. The same light t-shirt that is comfortable in a warmer climate can be the innermost layer in a colder climate.

REDUCE SOME MORE WEIGHT

43. LEAVE PRECIOUS THINGS AT HOME

Things that you would hate to lose or get damaged leave them at home. Precious jewelry, expensive gadgets or dresses, could be anything. You will not require these on your trip. Leave them at home and spare the load on your mind.

44. SEND SOUVENIRS BY MAIL

If you have spent all your money on purchasing souvenirs, carrying them back in the same bag that you brought along would be difficult. Either pack everything in another bag and check it in the airport or get everything shipped to your home. Use an international carrier for a secure transit, but this could be more expensive than the checking fees at the airport.

45. AVOID CARRYING BOOKS

Books equal to weight. There are many reading apps which you can download on your smart phone or tab.

>TOURIST

Plus there are gadgets like Kindle and Nook that are thinner and lighter alternatives to your regular book.

CHECK, GET, SET, CHECK AGAIN

46. STRATEGIZE BEFORE PACKING

Create a travel list and prepare all that you think you need to carry along. Keep everything on your bed or floor before packing and then think through once again – do I really need that? Any item that meets this question can be avoided. Remove whatever you don't really need and pack the rest.

47. TEST YOUR LUGGAGE

Once you have fully packed for the trip take a test trip with your luggage. Take your bags and go to town for window shopping for an hour. If you enjoy your hour long trip it is good to go, if not, go home and reduce the load some more. Repeat this test till you hit the right weight.

48. ADD A ROLL OF DUCT TAPE

You might wonder why, when this book has been talking about reducing stuff, we're suddenly asking you to pack something totally unusual. This is because when you have limited supplies, duct tape is immensely helpful for small repairs – a broken bag, leaking zip-lock bag, broken sunglasses, you name it and duct tape can fix it, temporarily.

49. LIST OF ESSENTIAL ITEMS

Even though the emphasis is on packing light, there are things which have to be carried for any trip. Here is our list of essentials:

- Passport/Visa or any other ID

- Any other paper work that might be required on a trip like permits, hotel reservation confirmations etc.

- Medicines – all your prescription medicines and emergency kit, especially if you are travelling with children

- Medical or vaccination records

- Money in foreign currency if travelling to a different country

- Tickets- Email or Message them to your phone

\>TOURIST

50. MAKE THE MOST OF YOUR TRIP

Wherever you are going, whatever you hope to do we encourage you to embrace it whole-heartedly. Take in the scenery, the culture and above all, enjoy your time away from home.

On a long journey even a straw weighs heavy.

-Spanish Proverb

>TOURIST

PACKING AND PLANNING TIPS

A Week before Leaving

- Arrange for someone to take care of pets and water plants.
- Stop mail and newspaper.
- Notify Credit Card companies where you are going.
- Change your thermostat settings.
- Car inspected, oil is changed, and tires have the correct pressure.
- Passports and photo identification is up to date.
- Pay bills.
- Copy important items and download travel Apps.
- Start collecting small bills for tips.

Right Before Leaving

- Clean out refrigerator.
- Empty garbage cans.
- Lock windows.
- Make sure you have the proper identification with you.
- Bring cash for tips.
- Remember travel documents.
- Lock door behind you.
- Remember wallet.
- Unplug items in house and pack chargers.

>TOURIST

READ OTHER GREATER THAN A TOURIST BOOKS

Greater Than a Tourist San Miguel de Allende Guanajuato Mexico: 50 Travel Tips from a Local by Tom Peterson

Greater Than a Tourist – Lake George Area New York USA: 50 Travel Tips from a Local by Janine Hirschklau

Greater Than a Tourist – Monterey California United States: 50 Travel Tips from a Local by Katie Begley

Greater Than a Tourist – Chanai Crete Greece: 50 Travel Tips from a Local by Dimitra Papagrigoraki

Greater Than a Tourist – The Garden Route Western Cape Province South Africa: 50 Travel Tips from a Local by Li-Anne McGregor van Aardt

Greater Than a Tourist – Sevilla Andalusia Spain: 50 Travel Tips from a Local by Gabi Gazon

Greater Than a Tourist – Kota Bharu Kelantan Malaysia: 50 Travel Tips from a Local by Aditi Shukla

Children's Book: Charlie the Cavalier Travels the World by Lisa Rusczyk

>TOURIST

> TOURIST

Visit Greater Than a Tourist for Free Travel Tips
http://GreaterThanATourist.com

Sign up for the Greater Than a Tourist Newsletter for discount days, new books, and travel information:
http://eepurl.com/cxspyf

Follow us on Facebook for tips, images, and ideas:
https://www.facebook.com/GreaterThanATourist

Follow us on Pinterest for travel tips and ideas:
http://pinterest.com/GreaterThanATourist

Follow us on Instagram for beautiful travel images:
http://Instagram.com/GreaterThanATourist

>TOURIST

> TOURIST

Please leave your honest review of this book on Amazon and Goodreads. Please send your feedback to GreaterThanaTourist@gmail.com as we continue to improve the series. We appreciate your positive and constructive feedback. Thank you.

>TOURIST

METRIC CONVERSIONS

TEMPERATURE

110° F — — 40° C
100° F —
90° F — — 30° C
80° F —
70° F — — 20° C
60° F —
50° F — — 10° C
40° F —
32° F — — 0° C
20° F —
10° F — — -10° C
0° F —
-10° F — — -18° C
-20° F — — -30° C

To convert F to C:

Subtract 32, and then multiply by 5/9 or .5555.

To Convert C to F:
Multiply by 1.8
and then add 32.

32F = 0C

LIQUID VOLUME

To Convert:............Multiply by
U.S. Gallons to Liters............... 3.8
U.S. Liters to Gallons 26
Imperial Gallons to U.S. Gallons 1.2
Imperial Gallons to Liters....... 4.55
Liters to Imperial Gallons 22
1 Liter = .26 U.S. Gallon
1 U.S. Gallon = 3.8 Liters

DISTANCE

To convert ....Multiply by
Inches to Centimeters 2.54
Centimeters to Inches 39
Feet to Meters...................... .3
Meters to Feet 3.28
Yards to Meters 91
Meters to Yards 1.09
Miles to Kilometers 1.61
Kilometers to Miles............ .62
1 Mile = 1.6 km
1 km = .62 Miles

WEIGHT

1 Ounce = .28 Grams
1 Pound = .4555 Kilograms
1 Gram = .04 Ounce
1 Kilogram = 2.2 Pounds

>TOURIST

TRAVEL QUESTIONS

- Do you bring presents home to family or friends after a vacation?
- Do you get motion sick?
- Do you have a favorite billboard?
- Do you know what to do if there is a flat tire?
- Do you like a sun roof open?
- Do you like to eat in the car?
- Do you like to wear sun glasses in the car?
- Do you like toppings on your ice cream?
- Do you use public bathrooms?
- Did you bring your cell phone and does it have power?
- Do you have a form of identification with you?
- Have you ever been pulled over by a cop?
- Have you ever given money to a stranger on a road trip?
- Have you ever taken a road trip with animals?
- Have you ever went on a vacation alone?
- Have you ever run out of gas?

- If you could move to any place in the world, where would it be?
- If you could travel anywhere in the world, where would you travel?
- If you could travel in any vehicle, which one would it be?
- If you had three things to wish for from a magic genie, what would they be?
- If you have a driver's license, how many times did it take you to pass the test?
- What are you the most afraid of on vacation?
- What do you want to get away from the most when you are on vacation?
- What foods smells bad to you?
- What item do you bring on ever trip with you away from home?
- What makes you sleepy?
- What song would you love to hear on the radio when you're cruising on the highway?
- What travel job would you want the least?
- What will you miss most while you are away from home?
- What is something you always wanted to try?

>TOURIST

- What is the best road side attraction that you ever saw?
- What is the farthest distance you ever biked?
- What is the farthest distance you ever walked?
- What is the weirdest thing you needed to buy while on vacation?
- What is your favorite candy?
- What is your favorite color car?
- What is your favorite family vacation?
- What is your favorite food?
- What is your favorite gas station drink or food?
- What is your favorite license plate design?
- What is your favorite restaurant?
- What is your favorite smell?
- What is your favorite song?
- What is your favorite sound that nature makes?
- What is your favorite thing to bring home from a vacation?
- What is your favorite vacation with friends?
- What is your favorite way to relax?

- Where is the farthest place you ever traveled in a car?
- Where is the farthest place you ever went North, South, East and West?
- Where is your favorite place in the world?
- Who is your favorite singer?
- Who taught you how to drive?
- Who will you miss the most while you are away?
- Who if the first person you will contact when you get to your destination?
- Who brought you on your first vacation?
- Who likes to travel the most in your life?
- Would you rather be hot or cold?
- Would you rather drive above, below, or at the speed limited?
- Would you rather drive on a highway or a back road?
- Would you rather go on a train or a boat?
- Would you rather go to the beach or the woods?

>TOURIST

TRAVEL BUCKET LIST

1.

2.

3.

4.

5.

6.

7.

8.

9.

10.

>TOURIST

NOTES

Made in the USA
Coppell, TX
29 June 2022